THE G.I. SERIES

Uncle Sam's Little Wars

The Spanish-American War,
Philippine Insurrection, and
Boxer Rebellion,
1898–1902

D1059898

The regimental sergeant major of the First U.S. Artillery. His rank is indicated by his scarlet chevrons with three arcs above three stripes points down outlined in black silk chain stitches. He wears the 1895-pattern forage cap and proper crossed cannon device without company letter as appropriate to his position. He has a triangular piece of kersey fabric added to his trouser cuffs to give them a wider flare or 'spring bottom' appearance. The trousers also display the proper 1-inch scarlet leg stripe of facing material.

THE G.I. SERIES

THE ILLUSTRATED HISTORY OF THE AMERICAN SOLDIER, HIS UNIFORM AND HIS EQUIPMENT

Uncle Sam's Little Wars

The Spanish-American War, Philippine Insurrection, and Boxer Rebellion, 1898–1902

John P. Langellier

Greenhill Books
LONDON
Stackpole Books
PENNSYLVANIA

Greenhill Books

*This book is dedicated to my cousin, George M. Langellier, Jr.,
who for decades has traveled many historic trails with me, in
good times and bad.*

Uncle Sam's Little Wars: The Spanish-American War, Philippine Insurrection, and Boxer Rebellion, 1898–1902
first published 1999 by Greenhill Books, Lionel Leventhal Limited, Park House, 1 Russell Gardens, London NW11 9NN
www.greenhillbooks.com
and
Stackpole Books, 5057 Ritter Road, Mechanicsburg, PA 17055, USA

British Library Cataloguing in Publication Data
Langellier, John P.
Uncle Sam's little wars: The Spanish-American War, Philippine Insurrection, and Boxer Rebellion, 1898-1902 - (G.I. The illustrated history of the American soldier, his uniform and his equipment ; v 15)
1. United States Army - History 2. United States. Army - Equipment 3. United States. Army - Uniforms 4. United States - History, Military
I. Title
355'00973

ISBN 1-85367-357-9

Library of Congress Cataloging-in-Publication Data
Langellier, J. Phillip.
Uncle Sam's little wars: The Spanish-American War, Philippine Insurrection, and Boxer Rebellion, 1898-1902 / by John P. Langellier.
        p. cm. -- (G.I. : 15)
ISBN 1-85367-357-9
1. Spanish-American War, 1898. 2. Philippines--History--Philippine American War, 1899-1902. 3. China--History--Boxer rebellion, 1899-1901. 4. United States--History, Military. 5. United States, Army--Uniforms--History--Pictorial Works. 6. United States, Army--Equipment--History--Pictorial Works
I. Title. II. Series: G.I. Series : 15.
E725.L36   1999
973.8'9--dc21   98-49195
                                            CIP

Designed by David Gibbons, DAG Publications Ltd
Layout by Anthony A. Evans
Edited by Donald Sommerville

Printed in Hong Kong

ACKNOWLEDGEMENTS AND ABBREVIATIONS
The author wishes to thank the following individuals and the staffs of the institutions listed below who are credited with the illustrations as follows:

DR	Dr Don Rickey, Jr.
FAM	Frontier Army Museum, Fort Leavenworth, KS
FSHM	Fort Sam Houston Museum, San Antonio, TX
FSM	Fort Sill Museum, Fort Sill, OK
GK	Gary Kurutz
GML	George M. Langellier, Jr.
ITC	Institute of Texan Culture, San Antonio, TX
JG	Jerome Greene
JMC	John M. Carroll
KHC	Kurt Hamilton Cox
LC	Library of Congress
MHS	Missouri Historical Society, St. Louis, MO
NA	National Archives, Washington, DC
PB	Peter Buxton
SHSW	State Historical Society of Wisconsin, Madison, WI
SI	Smithsonian Institution, Museum of American History
SM	Soldiers' Memorial, St Louis, MO
UK	University of Kansas Libraries, Joseph Pennell Collection, Kansas Collection, Lawrence, KS
USAQM	U.S. Army Quartermaster Museum, Fort Lee, VA
USAMHI	U.S. Army Military History Institute, Carlisle Barracks, PA
USA	U.S. Army, former Presidio Army Museum Collection, San Francisco, CA
USCM	U.S. Cavalry Museum, Fort Riley, KS
WCC	Western Costume Company, North Hollywood, CA

UNCLE SAM'S LITTLE WARS
THE SPANISH-AMERICAN WAR, PHILIPPINE INSURRECTION, AND BOXER REBELLION, 1898–1902

As the nineteenth century neared its close, one of the last remaining bastions of the once far-flung Spanish empire made its bid to leave His Catholic Majesty's fold. For years, Cuba had been in rebellion against the mother country and the conflict had gradually drawn international attention. Special scrutiny came from the United States where some sympathetic observers pictured the Cubans as freedom fighters waging a war for independence akin to the American Revolution.

In this climate of opinion the administrations of both President Grover Cleveland and that of his successor, William McKinley, attempted to bring the two sides together so they might resolve their differences peacefully. On 15 February 1898, however, hopes of a diplomatic solution disintegrated when the U.S.S. *Maine*, an American battleship then anchored in Havana Harbor, suddenly exploded with the loss of many lives. It is now generally believed that the explosion was the result of an accident, but this was not known at the time. The jingoists, as the war faction in the U.S. was sometimes known, blamed the Spanish and called for retaliation.

Less than a month later the U.S. Army gained two new artillery regiments, the Sixth and the Seventh, to augment the 28,183 men already under arms in the existing 25 infantry, ten cavalry, and five artillery regiments, all of which were at minimal strength. By April most of the foot soldiers and cavalrymen, along with ten batteries of field artillery had received orders to relocate from the various garrisons where they were posted (chiefly in the West) to marshaling areas that would allow them to deploy to Cuba.

Having set in motion the first stages of mobilization, Washington delivered an ultimatum to Madrid – abandon Cuba or face the consequences. On 21 April a declaration of war succeeded this weighty demand. Within two days Congress had authorized the president to call up 125,000 volunteers to support the regular army, and in May allowed a second call of 75,000 more fighting men.

While the United States had ample manpower, providing for a force nearly ten times larger than its peacetime predecessor taxed those entrusted with equipping, feeding, training, and tending to the medical as well as other needs of the gathering army. At first there was an insufficient supply of food and ammunition, and that which was available sometimes went astray, or had to be physically inspected to determine the contents of the many sealed, unmarked containers packed away in the scores of freight cars pouring into the staging camps.

The Spanish troops boasted Mauser rifles, smokeless powder magazine weapons that were state of the art at the time. The United States' answer, the .30-40 caliber Krag-Jörgensen rifle for infantrymen, and its carbine counterpart for cavalrymen, was in limited supply. Only 54,000 of the former and 15,000 of the latter weapons were on hand, meaning that most of these went to the regulars, while the volunteers often carried the old black powder, single-shot Springfield 'trapdoor'.

To heighten problems, no general staff existed to oversee preparations and direct operations. The preliminary plan called for the U.S. Army commanding general, Nelson Miles, to undertake the time-honored strategy of seizing the enemy capital, in this case Havana where a large Spanish army defended from strongly fortified positions. This concept went by the wayside when Admiral Pascual Cervera's Spanish Navy squadron crossed the Atlantic and steamed into the port at Santiago de Cuba.

The arrival of the Spanish fleet required a change in thinking. A U.S. Navy flotilla, commanded by Rear Admiral William Sampson, was called upon to blockade the harbor, while the

V Army Corps, commanded by the obese Civil War veteran and Medal of Honor recipient, William 'Pecos Bill' Shafter, was to sail from Tampa, Florida, and come ashore near Santiago to conduct land operations in support of the fleet. Shafter led eighteen regular and two volunteer infantry regiments, four light and two siege batteries of artillery, a machine gun company (chiefly Gatling guns), a squadron of regular mounted cavalry, and another ten squadrons of regular and two squadrons of volunteer cavalry, all of whom were dismounted. The last element included the 'Rough Riders,' who at first followed Colonel Leonard Wood, until this one-time physician turned field soldier gained a promotion and relinquished the unit to his second-in-command, Theodore Roosevelt.

Roosevelt's First Volunteer Cavalry and the others who constituted V Corps came from varied backgrounds, but they shared the common difficulties and confusion of embarkation. By 20 June they had arrived off Santiago, however, and as the convoy neared the end of its voyage, Daiquirí, a beach area twenty miles east of Santiago, was selected for debarkation. The landing was somewhat disorganized, but fortunately met with no enemy opposition. This was a stroke of good luck since some 33,000 Spaniards garrisoned the surrounding district. In fact, the only soldiers the Yankees encountered were friendly rebels, perhaps 4,000 or 5,000 of whom served under General Calixto Garcia. Garcia and Shafter met, exchanged intelligence, and agreed that they would work together, although no combined military operation ever emerged.

Instead, Shafter pressed on towards Santiago. The going was not easy with jungle impeding the advance. After some preliminary skirmishes, on 1 July Shafter moved against a village named El Caney and a series of ridges that would come to be known to history as San Juan Hill. Some 500 capable Spaniards held El Caney while another 1,200 were entrenched on the high ground. Although some 8,000 of Shafter's men faced them, the enemy's entrenched positions, extensive open fields of fire, and barbed wire obstacles presented formidable challenges. Compounding the predicament, narrow jungle paths were the safest means for the three attacking divisions to proceed but this slowed movement and wearied the U.S. troops and helped even the odds for the defenders.

The U.S. troops were from Joseph Wheeler's dismounted cavalry, and two infantry divisions, led by Henry Lawton and Jacob Kent. Despite their many disadvantages, Kent's command overwhelmed the key blockhouse on San Juan, while Wheeler's troopers gained the northern end of the ridge and Kettle Hill. At the same time, Lawton's foot soldiers took El Caney, then linked up with Wheeler's right. By then the attacking units were scattered and mixed, however, and halted instead of continuing their advance toward the Spaniards' second line of defense. On 2 July, therefore, the outcome of the battle remained in question, but during that day the exhausted adversaries exchanged fire with only limited results.

The next day, Admiral Cervera decided to run the American blockade. He hoisted anchor and led his squadron out to sea. This move brought disaster, for the U.S. fleet quickly destroyed the fleeing ships. With that, negotiations began, and on 17 July Santiago surrendered.

General Miles was not to be denied his place in this 'Splendid Little War' and sped toward Puerto Rico with 5,000 troops. Arriving with his advance party at Guánica, a southwestern point on the island, he took the Spanish commander by surprise since conventional wisdom was that the landing would be in the north near San Juan. Consequently, Miles faced only limited enemy resistance. Reinforcements quickly arrived and four separate columns moved from the south to the north by various routes. As in Cuba, the terrain and lack of roads kept the pace in low gear. Nonetheless, Miles was enjoying progress when word reached him that the Spanish had signed a peace protocol on 13 August. Puerto Rico was another prize that had been gained for what was effectively the growing U.S. empire.

There were equally dramatic victories on the other side of the globe. Admiral George Dewey commanded the U.S. Navy's Asiatic Squadron and when he heard of the declaration of war he set sail to strike Manila. On 1 May Dewey's force crushed the Spanish squadron at its base in Cavite in a swift decisive battle.

Dewey took over the base, but did not have the necessary personnel to disembark in order to capture and hold Manila. Reinforcements would have to come from over 6,000 miles away, a daunting distance given the transportation limitations of the time. Nonetheless, the first American troops, who had been gathering in the Bay Area, proceeded by sea from San Francisco on 25 May. It took them until 30 June to reach the Philippines. This lead group would subsequently be joined by other units so that by early August their commander, Major General Wesley Merritt, had 10,000 soldiers ashore. With supporting fire from the U.S. Navy Merritt moved toward Manila. The fighting was light, and the city fell on 13 August.

Fifteen days later Merritt departed with orders to make his way to Paris where peace negotiations had begun with the Spanish. General E.S. Otis assumed the reins of authority at that point, and forged ahead on a very difficult assignment, the establishment of a government for a dispersed series of 3,000 islands inhabited by 7,000,000 people of diverse cultures, religions, and languages unlike anything found in the United States.

Although the transition from Spanish to American authority in Cuba and Puerto Rico had been relatively smooth, the Philippine Islands did not go quietly into the new order of things. Filipinos had long opposed the Spanish and many of their leaders were heartened at first when the Spanish regime toppled. This optimism turned to disappointment in December 1898, after the peace terms between Spain and the United States ceded the islands to this new outside power.

It seemed that Washington was riding a second wave of 'Manifest Destiny'. Besides taking over Spanish colonial territory, the McKinley administration also annexed the Hawaiian Islands, an action which previously had been blocked by reluctant Democrats on the Hill and by other opponents, including the Japanese who contended that such a move would upset the status quo in the Pacific.

These objections fell by the wayside when U.S. officials realized the strategic importance of Hawaii, especially because of its position as a key link between the U.S. mainland and the Philippines. Indeed, on 1 June 1898 some 2,500 members of Merritt's Manila-bound army stopped briefly at Oahu where they received a warm reception. Within two weeks, the House, followed in July by the Senate, passed a joint resolution to accept Hawaii as a U.S. territory. Then the islands were quickly incorporated into the U.S. Army Department of California with the First New York Infantry Regiment and the Second Battalion U.S. Volunteer Engineers being dispatched in August to establish a post in Honolulu.

The implications of these proceedings were not lost on onlookers in the Philippines. Filipinos who desired to achieve autonomy from foreign rule now saw little difference between Spain and the United States. Relations became strained and an insurgency broke out, beginning with a 4 February 1899 incident when a group of armed Fil-ipinos drew fire from an American guard near Manila. An attack on the city came next, although this was repelled after two days of fighting with the loss of an estimated 3,000 Filipinos as opposed to 250 Americans. A possible uprising by the city's inhabitants did not break out as feared, a provost guard maintaining order even as a U.S. counter-attack drove off the Filipino forces. A similar clash took place at Iloilo, on the island of Panay, where American troops had been dispatched the previous December to occupy a former Spanish garrison.

The U.S. Army leadership lost little time in calling up fresh units, Otis' 12,000 men being seen as inadequate to face an enemy of as many as 40,000. Ten volunteer regiments were raised, and within seven months 35,000 reinforcements were on the way. The American high command in the islands went on the offensive even before all these reinforcements were available.

General Loyd Wheaton was dispatched with a mobile brigade to gain control of the Pasig River, a waterway that connected Laguna Bay with Manila Bay. Controlling it meant that the insurgents' territory would be cut in two. A combination of fortified garrisons and small army-manned gunboats basically brought about the desired results. The fighting did not end with this initiative though. The Filipinos battled on effectively using guerrilla tactics, though they were always short of weapons.

General Lawton, who had been transferred after the fighting in Cuba ceased, was dispatched to push into the Laguna basin while Wheaton forged ahead into Cavite Province, and the hill country between the China Sea and Laguna in the area referred to as the 'south line'. However, the 'north line' was the focal point of operations in that the provisional Filipino capital had been set up there 25 miles north of Manila at Malolos. This prize prompted the American commander in that area, General Arthur MacArthur (Douglas' father), to take decisive action.

He laid siege to Malolos, which capitulated on 31 March 1899. The Filipinos fled. MacArthur pursued, but the rugged terrain inhibited the chase. Undaunted, MacArthur pressed on toward San Fernando, prompting Emilio Aguinaldo, the redoubtable insurgent chief, to relocate his headquarters to Tarlac. There he braced himself for the coming onslaught.

After the rainy season passed, in fall 1899, and with new troops at their disposal, the American commanders again set out on a two-pronged offensive, with MacArthur fixing Tarlac as his objective and Lawton moving on the right. The path of Lawton's column was not as easily supplied as MacArthur's, meaning the men had to forage for supplies and make do with disintegrating clothing. Despite this, they persevered. Both drives succeeded and many of Aguinaldo's followers were subdued, although for the moment their leader escaped this fate.

In southern Luzon similar progress brought quiet there by March 1900, as was the case in the neighboring Visayas islands. But the end was not in sight yet. Between May 1900 and June 1901 some 1,000 separate clashes were recorded. Casualties mounted, but after Aguinaldo's capture in March 1901 by the tenacious, somewhat unorthodox brigadier general of volunteers, Fred Funston, the encounters decreased. With this the tense months of fighting ended. Except for occasional outbreaks over the next few years by such determined groups as the Moros the insurrection had run its course.

Even before the Philippine campaign had concluded, the islands became the stage for yet another drama. In China a wave of brutal sentiment against outsiders had gathered momentum in response to exploitation by ruthless 'foreign devils.' A secret society that came to be called the Boxers took up arms, and began to kill foreigners, including Christian missionaries, and some of their Chinese converts. The wave crested on 20 June 1900, when Boxers murdered the German minister to China in the streets of Peking, even as he was on his way to protest to the Imperial Chinese authorities in the Forbidden City about the wave of violence against foreigners.

Frightened that they would be next, many foreigners and Chinese Christians sought sanctuary in the legation compound (the section of Peking where the foreign embassies were situated) where they were soon besieged by Boxers and some elements of the Chinese Army. An international relief expedition was quickly mounted. Because the U.S. had a substantial force relatively close at hand in the Philippines, in less than three weeks after receiving their orders, the Ninth U.S. Infantry Regiment and a battalion of U.S. Marines landed at Dagu (also known as Taku), the port nearest Peking. In due course they were joined by Major General Adna Chaffee, who was in overall charge of the 2,500 Americans that eventually mobilized, placing this contingent third in number after the Russians and the Japanese.

With the forces of the combined powers in place, on 13 July American, British, French, Japanese, and Russian troops attacked Tianjin.

The walled city fell after a 15-hour engagement, opening the way to Peking, some 75 miles distant. By early August nearly 18,000 allied troops were in a position to march northward. The route was engulfed by Boxers and their sympathizers, and many skirmishes took place with serious losses. This did not deter the expedition's members. On 12 August they reached the gates of Peking, although the coalition then broke down since there was no supreme commander. Thus independent action was the order of the day at first, creating a certain degree of chaos.

Despite this, on 14 August the expedition reached the outer city. On that day two companies of the Fourteenth Infantry scaled the Tartar wall and gave covering fire to the British contingent who rushed into the city in force. The next day the final assault came, with a U.S. artillery unit known as 'Reilly's Battery' pounding down the gates to the Forbidden City – the seat of Chinese government. After some further mopping up action in the provinces, the international force withdrew in fall 1901, with the exception of a small contingent left behind to guard the legations.

So it was that less than four years after it had gone to war against Spain ill-prepared, the United States emerged as a major player on the international scene. Its army, which just a decade earlier had been little more than a frontier constabulary, was now a major military power with global responsibilities.

FOR FURTHER READING

Graham Cosmos, *An Army for Empire*.
  Columbia: University of Missouri Press, 1971.
John M. Gates, *Schoolbooks and Krags: The United States Army in the Philippines, 1898-1902*. Westport, CT: Greenwood Press, 1973.
Victor Purcell, *The Boxer Uprising*. New York: Cambridge University Press, 1963.
Russell Roth, *Muddy Glory: America's 'Indian Wars' in the Philippines 1899-1935*.
  W. Hanover, MA: The Christopher Publishing House, 1981.

From 1881 to 1902 a spiked helmet was the crowning glory on full dress occasions for company grade officers of heavy artillery and infantry, depicted (right) with scarlet trim for artillery and white for infantry. General officers continued to wear the *chapeau de bras*, as they had for decades, with major generals and above having the distinction of draping their sashes over the shoulder scarf style, while brigadier generals wore the buff sash tied around the waist.

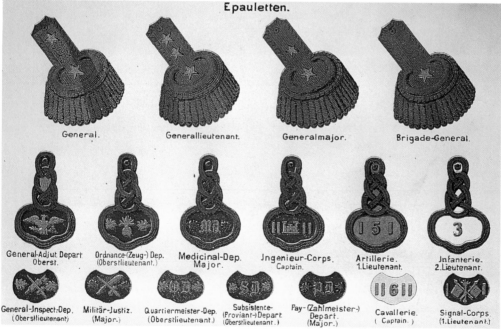

Above: From 1881 to 1902 mounted officers of artillery, cavalry, and infantry were to wear plumed helmets for dress occasions, with scarlet, yellow, or white plumes respectively. This included field grade officers, as well as adjutants and aides-de-camp. *Photograph by Gordon Chappell. LC*

Above: Company and field grade officers of artillery, cavalry, and infantry wore shoulder knots with scarlet-, yellow-, or white-faced pads on which the regimental number appeared in silver embroidery while the wearer's rank flanked the numeral, except for colonels whose silver-embroidered eagle appeared below. Dark blue backgrounds indicated the staff corps, with various devices such as a silver castle for engineers, a silver flaming bomb for the ordnance corps, and so forth appearing on the pad along with the rank. Note that, by the Spanish-American War, the 'MD' for medical officers shown in this illustration from a *circa* 1890 German publication, had been switched to a Maltese cross. The grade of general had been discontinued so that epaulets of the late 1890s for general officers had one, two, or three silver stars to indicate brigadier generals, major generals, and the Army's only lieutenant general. *Photograph by Gordon Chappell. LC*

Right: This color plate from the same German publication shows cloth chevrons for blouses and overcoats. They are, top row, left to right: quartermaster sergeant, hospital steward, acting hospital steward, cavalry chief trumpeter, infantry principal musician; middle row, left to right: infantry regimental and battalion color sergeant, artillery first sergeant, cavalry sergeant, engineer corporal, and the pre-1891 pattern Signal Corps device; bottom row, left to right: medical/hospital corps private, farrier, pioneer. *Photograph by Gordon Chappell. LC*

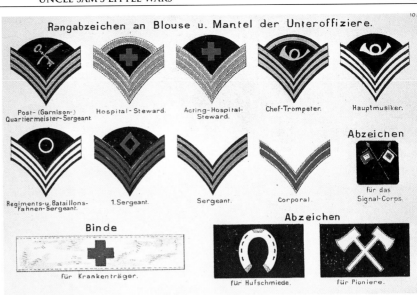

Centre right: Gold lace chevrons were worn on the dress coat as seen in the top row, from left to right, for an infantry principal musician, a cavalry saddler sergeant, an infantry regimental or battalion color sergeant, and a cavalry first sergeant. The middle row, from left to right, depicts the 1884-pattern gold lace chevrons for artillery sergeants, and infantry corporals, and service chevrons for peace as well as service chevrons for war or campaigns. The bottom row, left to right, depicts the cloth chevrons for an infantry sergeant major, artillery regimental quartermaster sergeant, post ordnance sergeant, commissary sergeant, and cavalry saddler sergeant. *Photograph by Gordon Chappell. LC*

Bottom right: In 1895 a round-topped forage cap with sloping visor was adopted for officers and enlisted men alike. The figure on the left wears the cap with the metallic dead and burnished wreath (ie dull gilt) with german silver Geneva cross appropriate for a hospital steward. His rank is further indicated by emerald green chevrons with a red cross above three stripes surmounted by an arc. The khaki uniform adopted in 1898 was worn with the campaign hat in most instances, and had detachable tabs that were in the color of the branch, such as white for infantry. A medium blue kersey overcoat with detachable cape was provided for cold weather, with the cape being lined in branch colors, scarlet being the designating shade for artillery. Note the chevrons for this artillery sergeant (center) appear below the elbows, while those on the blouse were to appear above the elbows, as seen for the infantry sergeant on the far right. Brown canvas leggings were another addition to the field uniform starting in 1887.

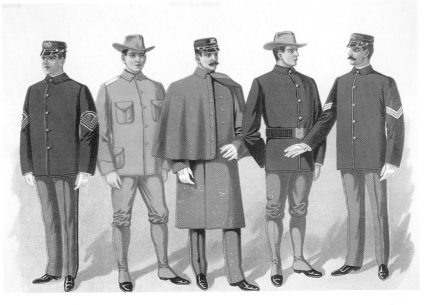

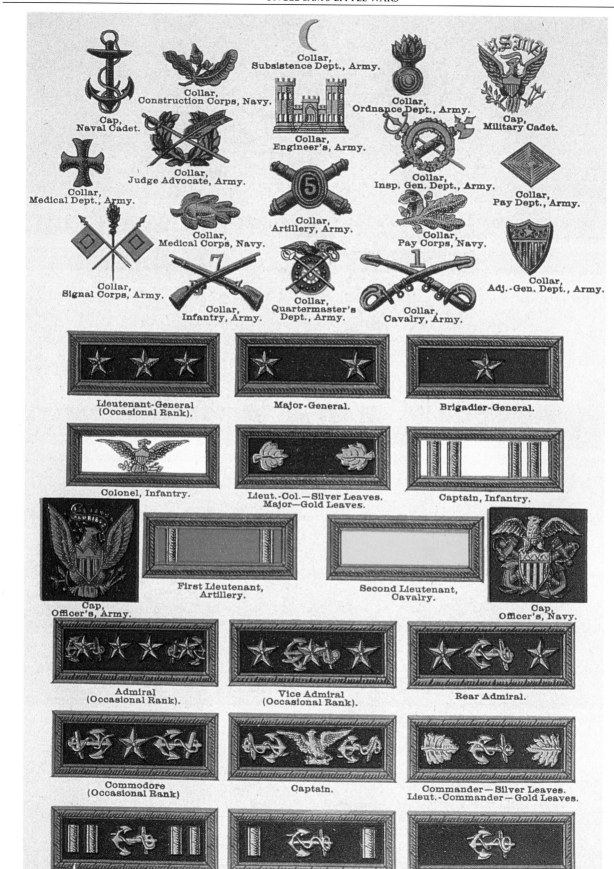

Cap,
Naval Cadet.

Collar,
Construction Corps, Navy.

Collar,
Subsistence Dept., Army.

Collar,
Ordnance Dept., Army.

Cap,
Military Cadet.

Collar,
Engineer's, Army.

Collar,
Medical Dept., Army.

Collar,
Judge Advocate, Army.

Collar,
Insp. Gen. Dept., Army.

Collar,
Pay Dept., Army.

Collar,
Medical Corps, Navy.

Collar,
Artillery, Army.

Collar,
Pay Corps, Navy.

Collar,
Adj.-Gen. Dept., Army.

Collar,
Signal Corps, Army.

Collar,
Infantry, Army.

Collar,
Quartermaster's
Dept., Army.

Collar,
Cavalry, Army.

Lieutenant-General
(Occasional Rank).

Major-General.

Brigadier-General.

Colonel, Infantry.

Lieut.-Col.—Silver Leaves.
Major—Gold Leaves.

Captain, Infantry.

Cap,
Officer's, Army.

First Lieutenant,
Artillery.

Second Lieutenant,
Cavalry.

Cap,
Officer's, Navy.

Admiral
(Occasional Rank).

Vice Admiral
(Occasional Rank).

Rear Admiral.

Commodore
(Occasional Rank)

Captain.

Commander—Silver Leaves.
Lieut.-Commander—Gold Leaves.

Lieutenant.

Lieutenant,
Junior Grade.

Ensign.

Left: This illustration shows a selection of U.S. Army and Navy collar devices and shoulder straps of the late nineteenth century. The army shoulder straps indicated the officer's branch, as did collar devices for the blouse. These items were either embroidered or of metal simulated to appear as gold or silver embroidery. The color of the shoulder strap backing was also indicative of branch, while the silver bars, gold and silver oak leaves, silver eagles, and silver stars indicated rank.

Above: A number of field blouses were prescribed late in the nineteenth century. For instance, the infantry colonel, front left, wears the officer's 1895-pattern with concealed buttons and mohair trim while in the center a brigadier general's 1898-pattern field blouse appears in contrast to the single-breasted five-button sack coat of the post electrician sergeant of the style adopted by 1884 and which remained in use into the early 1900s (right). Two officers in the background have on the officer's white summer uniform with the shoulder loops added to the garment in 1901. Note that the brigadier general has opted to don the black campaign hat which was still permitted, but not preferred by most individuals of the period. *WCC*

The original 1898-pattern khaki uniform blouse had a stand collar for officers and enlisted men alike. For officers, the branch-colored shoulder loops were attached permanently to the jacket. White designated infantry, black the staff, yellow cavalry, and so forth. The khaki cork summer helmet covered in drilling was one option for field wear in the tropics, following British colonial examples. The 1899-pattern drab campaign hat with large screen mesh vents in the crown was the more common headpiece, however. Intermixed gold and black hat cords were authorized for officers. *WCC*

Right: The array of 1898–1902 artillery uniforms included, from left to right: light artillery sergeant; heavy artillery private in khaki uniform equipped as infantry; artillery colonel in khaki field uniform; brigadier general in 1898-pattern blue serge field service blouse; staff officer; major general full dress; heavy artillery company grade officer full dress; light artillery officer full dress; heavy artillery private full dress; light artillery sergeant full dress. *WCC*

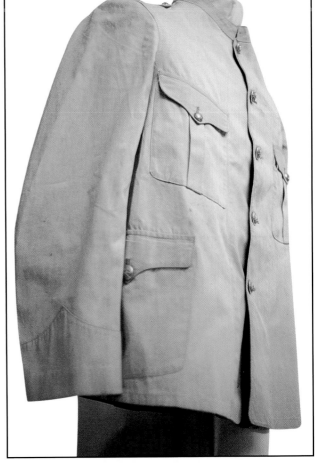

Above: The first 1898-pattern khaki blouses were to have the pocket flaps, cuffs, and collar covered in material of branch, but in reality this practice was carried out mostly by volunteers and guardsmen, not regulars, as this example for a volunteer infantryman depicts. *JG*

Above: Some khaki blouses did not have the lower pocket flaps covered. The materials for this decoration varied as well. For instance, inexpensive yellow felt was applied to this cavalry jacket, which once again was more likely than not made for the use of a volunteer. *USCM*

Left: The detachable black shoulder loop with white piping for the Signal Corps worn on the 1899-pattern khaki jacket. *JG*

Below: Officers below the rank of colonel were to have their branch device on either side of the collar with either a 'US' for regulars or a 'USV' for United States Volunteers in front. This example was worn by a lieutenant colonel of the Third Wisconsin infantry. The rank insignia was a silver oak leaf. Above this is attached the proper 1898-pattern gilt Arms of the United States. The color, albeit faded, is light blue for infantry, although in the case of regulars the infantry had white facings. *SHSW*

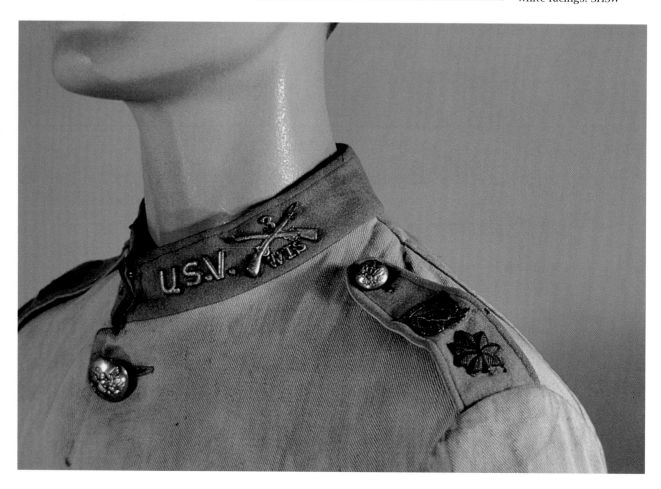

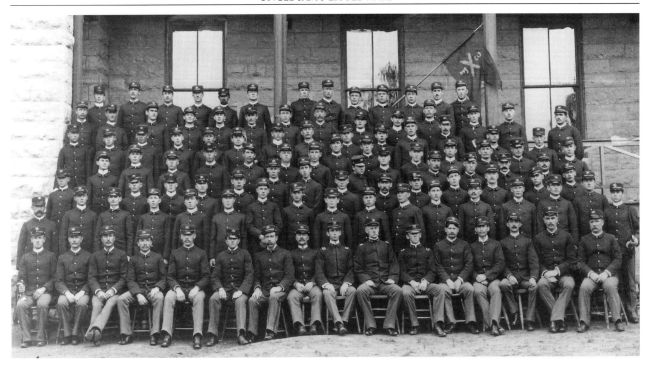

Above: Light Battery F, Third U.S. Artillery, a designation easily ascertained by the scarlet 1889-pattern guidon with the yellow applied battery letter and regimental number above and below the yellow crossed cannon. The men wear the garrison uniform as it was prescribed from 1895–1902. Their cap insignia has both the regimental number and battery letter as called for in the case of company, troop, or battery enlisted personnel. *UK*

Below: Some members of Troop F, First U.S. Cavalry, relax in their garrison uniforms. Most wear white dress collars under their blouses, although the man on the porch to the left with a riding crop or cane wears an 1883-pattern dark blue issue shirt. *UK*

Left: John Jefferson was a trumpeter in Troop D, Tenth U.S. Cavalry, one of the famed 'buffalo soldier' regiments. He appears in the typical garrison uniform of the late nineteenth century, including 1895-pattern forage cap with its cast regulation one-piece brass crossed saber device that had the regimental number above and troop letter below. These were held on the cap by a screwpost with a round nut. The double ½-inch leg stripes of yellow facing material, officially adopted in 1883, further indicated his status as a musician. Note the marksmanship device on his chest as well. *Mrs John Jefferson, ITC*

Below: Corporal Merrill of Troop B, Fourth U.S. Cavalry, depicts the finely tailored look of the five-button enlisted blouse that was far more form-fitting by the late 1880s than previous models. Note the two stripes on his sleeves indicating his rank. *UK*

Above: From 1897 enlisted men of the Hospital Corps were no longer issued dress uniforms. Instead, the 1895-pattern cap and five-button blouse served for both garrison and dress occasions. As a consequence, these 'medics' were authorized service chevrons, such as seen on the hospital steward seated in the front row center, of emerald green piped in white chain stitching for two enlistments in peacetime. The private in the rear row far right appears to have on service-in-war chevrons, which were green trimmed in orange. *FSHM*

Below: An acting hospital steward, seated in the right foreground wearing the 1887-pattern three emerald green chevrons outlined in white chain stitching surmounted by a red Geneva cross, poses in a hospital ward with a few other fellow medical personnel and their patients. *UK*

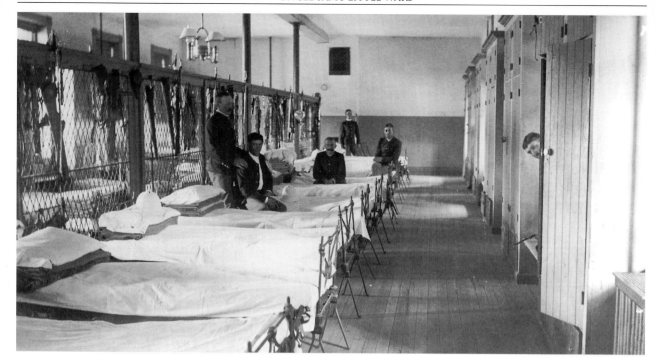

Above: The iron 1870–71 'composite bunk' No. 9 is evident in this late 1890s' barracks scene at Fort Riley, Kansas. The wall lockers were a late Victorian era improvement over the smaller footlocker. Note that these men have hung their carbine scabbards, sabers and other equipment from the wire mesh that runs down the center of the room. *UK*

Below: Again the troopers in this Fort Riley, Kansas, barracks have used the center mesh to hang M1859 Light Cavalry Sabers and other gear. The bunks are the new model introduced between 1893 and 1895, while M1875 foot-lockers are placed at the end of each one. It seems that wall lockers or half-wall lockers were also provided for these troops of the late 1890s. *USCM*

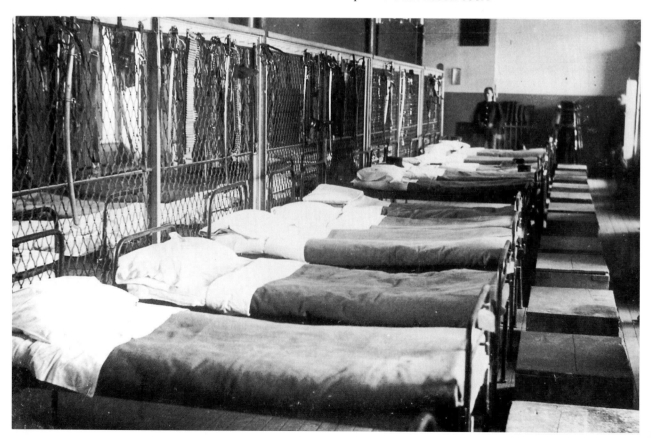

Above: Men of the First U.S. Cavalry, at San Carlos, Arizona Territory, in the 1890s, prepare a meal in the company kitchen. The 'waiter' wears a dark blue vest which was permitted by regulations as optional. The white canvas trousers had also been introduced just a few years earlier, and served in hot weather or for such work as kitchen duty, later referred to as KP, a slang term for kitchen police. *USCM*

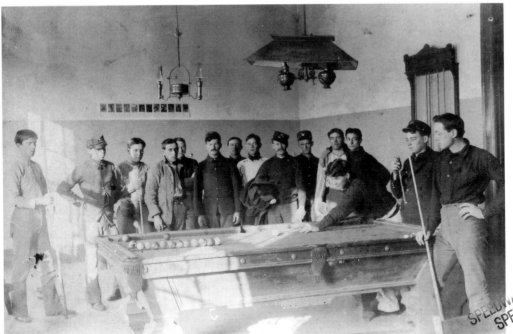

Left: Turn of the century artillerymen at Fort Leavenworth, Kansas, engage in a game of pocket billiards. They all have the light or medium blue kersey trousers, but wear various outer garments from regulation five-button blouses to privately purchased civilian shirts. *FAM*

Above: Four Eighth U.S. Cavalry troopers depict the variations of the common garrison uniform as it existed in the later 1890s, including the five-button blouse worn with the 1895-pattern forage cap, and the 1889-pattern drab campaign hat. Trousers were either the medium blue kersey 1885 pattern or the white cotton duck summer trousers of either the 1888 or 1889 pattern, both these types replacing the previous linen styles prescribed in 1885. *USCM*

Right: Apache Scouts at San Carlos, Arizona Territory, wear the 1889-pattern drab campaign hat rather than the 1890-pattern black round-crown hat that was called for as a distinct item of their uniform. The guidon at the left is the special Indian Scout model, however, that bore a crossed arrows device. Chevrons on the first sergeant and corporal who flank the guidon may be the 1890-pattern white with red piping for Indian Scout non-commissioned officers, or possibly 1884-pattern infantry chevrons which were white with black chain stitching. *NA*

Left: A corporal of Troop D, Second Cavalry, turns out in the garrison uniform complete with the pebble-grained leather high top boots adopted in the mid-1880s. He wears marksmanship devices on his collar and the left breast and has on the gauntlets which began to be issued to enlisted men in the early 1880s. The stripes on his trousers were to be ½-inch in yellow facing material, while two stripes on the sleeves of his five-button blouse, likewise in yellow facing material outlined in black stitching, further indicated his rank. The M1859 Light Cavalry Saber slung on the left side of his horse with saber straps has the M1885 saber knot affixed to the guard. Note the 'fender' or sweat leather that has been attached to the stirrup straps of what is either an M1885 McClellan saddle or the M1896 version. *UK*

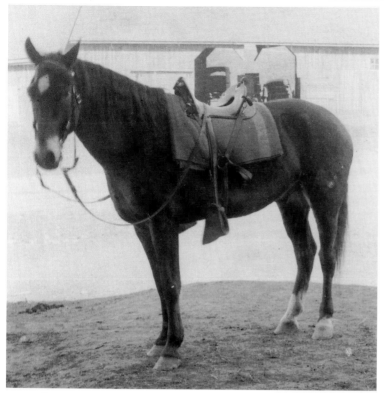

Left: A cavalry mount with what is either the M1885 McClellan saddle or the so-called 'Godfrey' modification introduced in 1896 to alter how the quarterstraps and girth straps were fitted. Also evident is the gray saddle blanket with yellow stripe that began to be issued in the late 1870s, and the M1885 bridle with M1892 bit, all typical for the cavalryman of the late 1890s. For the most part, the cavalry units sent to Cuba and the first ones dispatched to the Philippines went without their mounts. *UK*

Below: Two new weapons were coming into the hands of the U.S. Cavalry late in the nineteenth century, the M1896 .38 caliber Colt double-action revolver and the M1896 Krag carbine, both seen here as the armament for this private. The early version of the cavalry Krag had a saddle ring which meant that the M1885 carbine sling could be hooked up with the weapon even though it was secured in a long scabbard. Note that the M1874 'Shoemaker' bit is still in use rather than the new M1892. *NA*

Above: The Krag carbine was a smokeless powder magazine weapon that was in the hands of regular army troopers at the outbreak of the Spanish-American War, but was not issued to all militiamen and volunteers. *GML*

Below: The scabbard for the Krag was moved to the left side of the horse in the late 1890s, thereby causing the saber to be shifted to the right side. This edged weapon was more symbolic than practical by this period, but conservative military leaders were not ready to abandon this long-time cavalry arm. *UK*

Left: All these men from the First Cavalry have placed their sabers on the right side to accommodate their carbine scabbards on the left. They all have blue canvas Mills cartridge belts to carry rounds both for their carbines and also their .38 revolvers. *UK*

Opposite page, bottom: Men of Troop C, Second U.S. Cavalry, all have their saddle ring M1896 Krag carbines. Note that the soldier standing in the rear row second from the left has opened the bolt of his carbine. They also all wear mounted reinforced kersey trousers, the 1883-pattern field shirt, and the 1889-pattern campaign hat. *UK*

Below: Brown canvas 1888- or 1889-pattern leggings had begun to replace boots for field and campaign wear by the late 1890s, as indicated by the two privates in the right foreground. *UK*

Opposite page, top: More and more men began to wear belts with their trousers in the 1890s, as the private from Troop K, First U.S. Cavalry, does in the center of this photograph. His 'bunkie' to his right has on white canvas 1889-pattern mounted overalls and an undershirt which may be the regulation pattern with the sleeves cut down. The seated man has on the unaltered long sleeve 1881-pattern undershirt. *UK*

Opposite page, bottom: The undershirt was combined with the white canvas mounted overalls and the 1879-pattern stable frock of white canvas for certain fatigue chores and stable duty as is evident with this group from Troop D, Second U.S. Cavalry. *UK*

Above: Mounted artillerymen were basically issued the same uniform as their comrades in the cavalry, except that the scarlet branch color was used for chevrons and trouser stripes, as can be seen in the case of the sergeant mounted on the lead horse. Further, the men do not have the M1840 Light Artillery Saber slung from their saddles, but instead wear them from their M1885 saber belts. In addition, rather than the gray saddle blanket, they have dark blue saddle cloths trimmed in red. Finally, note that the gunner in the rear has metal stirrups rather than the wooden cavalry model covered with black harness leather. *NA*

Below: Gun drill for Light Battery F, Second U.S. Artillery, where the gunners stand next to their 3.2-inch breech-loading 'bag guns', the main field piece for the regular army horse artillery of the late Victorian era. The man on the far right wears a fuze pouch on his right hip, while the artilleryman directly in front of him wears the old M1851 eagle buckle with applied German silver wreath, rather than the rectangular brass plate with US that was the norm by the late nineteenth century for enlisted men. A mixture of accoutrements and uniforms from different eras remained a fact of army life, although this combination was less common in the late 1890s than it had been previously. *UK*

Left: A white cap cover for the 1895-pattern forage cap was also provided and could be combined with the white cotton duck 1888- or 1889-pattern summer trousers and the white cotton five-button sack coat, also specified in 1888 and later changed slightly in 1889. This ensemble was a welcome relief during hot weather. *NA*

Right: Private John Schillelin of Battery F, Third U.S. Artillery, is prepared for a colder climate in his 1889-pattern sky blue kersey enlisted overcoat with detachable cape. The lining of the cap was scarlet for artillery and engineers, dark blue for infantry, medium yellow for cavalry, crimson for ordnance personnel, emerald green for medical personnel, buff for quartermaster sergeants, and gray for commissary sergeants. Note the leather pistol cartridge pouch worn on the M1885 saber belt in front of the butt-forward revolver. *UK*

Below: Cavalrymen have turned their capes back to reveal the yellow lining in this scene in front of the guardhouse at Fort Riley, Kansas. The overcoat could be worn without the cape when not under arms. *USCM*

Above: The cape was held on to the overcoat with hooks and eyes, thereby making it possible to remove it and wear it over the blouse without the overcoat. Once again, this is an artilleryman and thus the cape lining is scarlet.

Above right: Officers likewise had overcoats, but these were heavy dark blue ulsters with black mohair frogging. Rank was indicated by black mohair soutache braid that was supposed to be ⅛-inch in width. This braid was applied above the cuff with a plain sleeve for second lieutenants, one knot for first lieutenants, and so forth up to five knots for colonels. This man is a major who wears the typical headdress for this garment, the 1895-pattern officer's undress cap, although the overcoat could be worn with the campaign hat. *UK*

Left: A dark blue cape trimmed in ½-inch black braid, with a black velvet rolling collar and black mohair loop was permitted for use over the blouse or the officer's overcoat. Dark blue lining was specified for general and staff officers, scarlet for artillery, yellow for cavalry, and white for infantry, as seen here for this second lieutenant who cradles an M1860 staff and field officer's sword. The cape partially covers his 1895-pattern officer's undress coat. *UK*

Right: The officer's 1895-pattern undress coat had a stand collar covered in black mohair that bore either embroidered branch devices and the letters 'U.S.' or metallic simulated embroidered insignia, the latter case being illustrated by this first lieutenant of the Third U.S. Cavalry. His rank is indicated by shoulder straps with yellow centers and with a single silver bar at each end. *USCM*

Left: This acting assistant surgeon wears simulated embroidered collar insignia, too, in this case a gold Maltese cross which was adopted in 1896 for medical officers. The shoulder straps had dark blue centers bordered by gold embroidery, while the bars indicating rank were silver.

Opposite page, top: The 1895-pattern blouse for infantry officers exhibited crossed rifles with the regiment above, in this case the number '20' that also appears on the saddle cloth in white to match the cloth's trim. Despite the fact that infantrymen were afoot, their field grade officers were often mounted as were the regimental adjutants. These officers could often obtain cavalry boots and gauntlets, and in this instance even an M1872 light cavalry officer's saber. Note that the saber straps on the belt are connected to a single hanger at the waist. Earlier versions of officer's belts had two separate straps. *NA*

Opposite page, bottom: Colonel Abraham Arnold, commanding the First Cavalry, wears leggings rather than boots with his undress coat and 1895-pattern undress cap. The black mohair trim that adorns the front and skirts of the coat can be seen as can the side

Left: The saber belt was worn under the 1895-pattern officer's undress coat. For field situations the undress cap could be replaced by a drab or black campaign hat for officers, although those for enlisted men were universally of the drab type. The light blue trousers are set off by 1½-inch yellow stripes of facing material, the mark of a cavalry officer dating back to 1872. *NA*

Left: Cavalry officer's trouser stripes are also seen clearly for this Third U.S. Cavalry subaltern in his full dress uniform of the 1881–1902 era. The buffalo or yak plume was to be yellow as were the centers of the pads on his dress knots. *NA*

Above: Regimental adjutants and aides-de-camp suspended aiguillettes from the right shoulders of their dress uniforms. This officer has selected a Whitman saddle, rather than the more common McClellan type. *UK*

Right: Private Jesse Harris, Troop D, Seventh U.S Cavalry, turns out in the dress uniform of a cavalry trooper. The coat is the 1887 pattern with dark yellow facings. He wears the black high-topped boots that had come to be associated with cavalrymen. *DR*

Above: Boots for dress wear began to be replaced in certain instances by brown canvas leggings as a private from Troop C, Fourth U.S. Cavalry, demonstrates in this portrait. His helmet cords are worn incorrectly. Once again, the Krag carbine is seen in its scabbard, but located on the right side rather than left. Placement of this weapon on the saddle varied according to a number of factors. *UK*

Left: Gold lace chevrons were adopted in 1884 for dress uniforms of non commissioned officers, as this regimental quartermaster sergeant of the Twentieth U.S. Infantry demonstrates. The chevrons were backed in branch colors, such as white for infantry. Service stripes on dark blue backings were also prescribed for regular enlistments and with branch colored backings when an individual had served in wartime or on certain campaigns. A leather frog attached to the waist belt with cast U.S. plate holds the M1840 Non-Commissioned Officer's Sword. *NA*

Right: Bandsmen and musicians had herringbones of branch color on the front of their dress coats and could also wear additional accessories such as the yellow shoulder knots with attached mohair cords, and a triple gold cord with tassels and flounders. The helmet plate of this cavalry regimental bandsman's 1881-pattern plumed helmet with yellow horsetail plume and matching worsted cords bears a German silver lyre. *UK*

Above: By the mid-1890s infantrymen in the regular army had given up their old .45-70 black powder single-shot Springfields for the .30-40 Krag, a magazine weapon that fired smokeless powder cartridges.

Below: In 1895 the leather belt with rectangular brass buckle began to be discontinued, even for full dress. Blue canvas Mills cartridge belts were to be worn in a rather incongruous mixture as of that year for troops armed with the Krag rifle. *USA*

Bottom of page: Soon after the sinking of U.S.S. *Maine* regulars put aside their dress uniforms, shouldered their Krags, and marched off to join their volunteer comrades for a war against Spain. Here men of the Twenty-fifth U.S. Infantry Regiment, a unit composed of black enlisted men, follow the regimental colors and standard in their 1889-pattern campaign hats. The soldiers have Mills belts for .30 caliber cartridges, the Krag and bayonet, knapsack, shelter half, and haversack, over the dark blue wool blouse. *NA*

Below: Another means of carrying necessities to the field dating back to the Civil War was the 'blanket roll,' as employed by these infantrymen who mobilized to fight the Spanish in Cuba. *NA*

Bottom of page: The call to arms went out and thousands of men responded. Here, in a staged scene from 1898, recruits are issued their brand new dark blue five-button wool blouses, light blue kersey trousers, 1889-pattern campaign hats, and other items of their field kit, although much of the issue was not suitable for use in the climates where they were to be sent. *NA*

Left: When the First U.S. Volunteer Cavalry, better known as the 'Rough Riders,' reported for duty in San Antonio, Texas, uniforms were in short supply. At first some of the men of the unit were issued the 1884-pattern brown duck sack coats with matching trousers that had been adopted by the regular army for fatigue purposes. This private from the unit has on such an outfit that one of his comrades unflatteringly recalled as 'stinking brown jeans.' *FSHM*

Below left: Enlisted Rough Riders eventually put aside the 1884-pattern brown duck jacket and in the main wore the 1883-pattern blue flannel pullover shirt with the 1889-pattern drab campaign hat as seen here for the men of Company H. Also note the exposed suspenders (braces), which in previous times were seldom seen when the blouse was not worn.

Opposite page, top: The most prominent Rough Rider, Teddy Roosevelt, also occasionally wore his suspenders over the field shirt, although he preferred khaki trousers to the issue blue kersey ones worn by most of his men. The trooper seated immediately to T.R.'s right has substituted custom leggings, perhaps of leather, for the issue brown canvas versions. *LC*

Opposite page, bottom: Two infantry officers look on from the left as men offload a train during mobilization prior to departure for Cuba. The officers wear the stand collar mohair blouse adopted in 1895, and their trousers exhibit the 1½-inch wide white stripes down the outer seams as was proper for the infantry. Another officer, center right adjusting his hat, has removed his blouse and wears the field shirt. *NA*

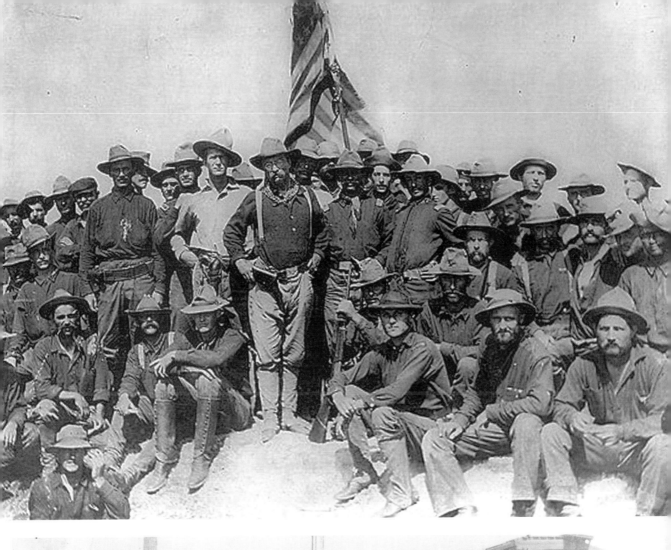

Above: While forces gathered in the South for duty in Cuba, other units bound for the Philippines assembled in the West, especially around the San Francisco Bay area, as these volunteers did. Note that the old 1872-pattern forage cap is being worn by most of the enlisted men of this volunteer infantry company, save for the sergeant on the right and the fifers and drummers on the left. Once again, the old blue wool uniform is in use, despite its inappropriateness for the climate of the Philippines where the troops were to be deployed. *USA*

Below: Even these regulars from Battery O, Sixth U.S. Artillery, at the Presidio of San Francisco continued in the hot wool uniform. Their field pieces are 3.2-inch M1897 breech-loaders, the most up-to-date light artillery pieces in the U.S. inventory of the era, although they fired black powder rather than smokeless charges. *USA*

Above: These volunteer infantrymen from Tennessee also had weapons that fired black powder, in this case Springfield .45-70 rifles from the 1880s, complete with their leather slings. *USA*

Right: This volunteer from one of the New York infantry regiments likewise carries a .45-70 Springfield, but one of the later ramrod bayonet models. The 'N.Y.' on his stamped brass Mills belt plate and the embroidered 'N.Y.' on his 1883 pattern shirt indicate his origins. *USA*

Opposite page: The Second U.S. Volunteer Engineer Regiment left the Bay area for Pacific duty, but not in the Philippines. They were sent to establish an American presence in Hawaii in 1898. The khaki Mills belt is seen here for .45-70 cartridges for their trapdoor Springfields. The sergeant on the left displays the scarlet leg stripes piped in white and scarlet chevrons with white silk chain stitch that were proper for engineer NCOs. The man on the right wears civilian suspenders. *PB*

Right: William Borthwick, on the left, was an artificer corporal with the First Montana Infantry. There was no such rank in the regular army, only artificers being authorized and designated by slightly smaller crossed hammers than seen here. Borthwick also has pronounced white stitching at the top of his chevrons and wears gold service stripes, as does his unknown comrade. Once again, enlisted regulars did not wear bullion service stripes on their five-button blouses, but only on their dress coats. *SM*

Below: As the Fifty-first Iowa march off to awaiting transports to take them from San Francisco to Manila, they, too, have the wool two-tone blue uniform and .45-70 Springfield. They carry their rolled shelter halves above what appear to be M1878 blanket bags. The officer in the right foreground has two emblems on his chest, one of which seems to be an VIII Corps badge. Corps badges had been discontinued after the Civil War, but were reinstituted in a new form for the Spanish American War. *USA*

Above: While some of the men remained behind in Cuba after Spain's treaty of peace, most of the 'Boys in Blue' returned to their homes, such as these Kansans who receive a warm welcome from the local citizenry. *UK*

Below: As one means of dealing with the climate of the Philippines some of the men from the First California Volunteer Infantry Regiment opted for white trousers, presumably of cotton, in lieu of the sky-blue wool issue garment. *USA*

Opposite page: These foot soldiers in the far away Philippine Islands retained the light blue kersey trousers and 1883-pattern dark blue flannel shirt, although this pair of infantrymen have the Krag rifle, with the bayonet developed for this weapon, rather than outmoded Springfields. The man on the right wears an unauthorized medal, which may be some sort of marksmanship device or custom unit insignia. *USAMHI*

Right: The summer version of the 1895-pattern officer's blouse was white as were the trousers. No insignia of any sort was prescribed at first with this jacket. Various types of headgear could be combined with this uniform, including the 1889-pattern campaign hat. *SI*

Left: During 1898 a dark blue serge field service blouse was also provided as an option for officers' field wear. The same shoulder straps authorized for the 1895-pattern officer's blouse were to be used, plain ones with white centers designating the branch and rank of Second Lieutenant William Parker, an officer with the Eleventh U.S. Infantry, as indicated by his metallic collar insignia. *USA*

Major Drew, a member of the Adjutant General's Corps of the Tennessee Volunteer Guard, displays the dark blue 1898-pattern serge field service blouse with four exterior pockets. His plain trousers without stripe or welt are of matching material to the jacket as was regulation for staff officers, while infantry, cavalry, and artillery officers had sky-blue trousers with 1½-inch leg stripes made of facing material in branch colors. *UK*

Above: These regulars all have the 1898-pattern khaki blouse, except for Colonel Arthur Wagner of the Adjutant General's Corps, who has opted for the 1898 pattern officer's blue serge blouse. Note that the collars and cuffs of regular army officer's jackets were plain; only the shoulder loops were color-coded according to branch, unlike the jackets of many volunteers. *NA*

Right: Originally the blouses of regulars were to have the cuffs, shoulder loops, and collar faced in branch color, as Private Barnhardt, a member of the newly formed Seventh U.S. Artillery, models here. Note the 1898-pattern enlisted man's artillery scarlet hat cords on his campaign hat and the crossed cannon insignia, which designate his unit and branch. Such insignia, while at first intended for use with the 1895-pattern enlisted forage cap, were frequently attached to the campaign hat as well. *UK*

Opposite page: Officers of the regular army and most volunteers usually followed the prescribed means of depicting their rank on the khaki blouse by means of shoulder loops that were of branch color, in this case scarlet piped in white for engineers, with a single silver bar for first lieutenants, two silver bars for captains, a gold oak leaf for majors, a silver oak leaf for lieutenant colonels, and a spread eagle for colonels. Generals had five-pointed stars. Also, first lieutenants through lieutenant colonels were to display the Coat of Arms of the United States on the loops while colonels were to place them on their collars. *FAM*

Left: This infantry private wears the enlisted version of the khaki jacket with stand collar and white shoulder loops of the type called for in July 1898 by the secretary of war, which abandoned the more costly, complicated facing color scheme for the collar and cuffs. The soldier also wears khaki trousers. *USA*

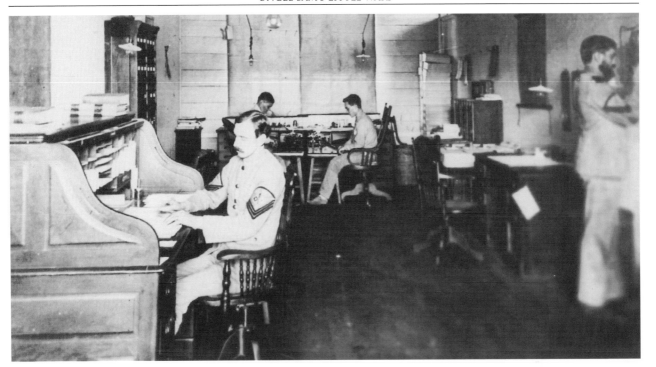

Above: The enlisted khaki blouse as it came to exist after July 1898 had detachable shoulder loops to facilitate laundering and also to make it possible to mass produce the garments more easily, then add the appropriate loops, such as black piped in white for the Signal Corps as depicted here. The khaki uniform saw only limited use during the Cuban and Puerto Rican campaigns and the early fighting in the Philippines. *NA*

Right: Even when khaki blouses were not worn, the trousers or breeches might be combined with the 1883-pattern blue shirt as a campaign uniform, along with the drab hat. Note that in July 1898 numbers and letters were adopted, along with hat cords, in this case yellow for cavalry. *USCM*

Left: Because the khaki trousers and breeches of regulars did not display the traditional ½-inch trouser stripes for corporals and 1-inch trouser stripes for sergeants through sergeants major, some non-commissioned officers began to apply chevrons to their shirts during the Spanish-American War. This heretofore unknown practice received official approval in 1898. Note that the cavalry sergeant photographed here has simply pinned his chevrons above the elbows. *USCM*

Opposite page, top: The 1872-pattern chevron for the blouse, overcoat, and khaki jacket were rather large for the shirt with its tighter sleeves. Consequently, some non-commissioned officers cut their chevrons down or had smaller custom ones made, as did the sergeant in this group of cavalrymen in the Philippines standing behind a Colt 'potato digger' machine gun. In 1900 smaller chevrons were adopted as standard for shirts, and two years later the first specification for these insignia appeared. *USA*

Opposite page, bottom: In 1899 the rank of electrician sergeant was created for the coast artillery, and a special insignia comprising white embroidered lighting bolts above three scarlet chevrons with white chain stitches was adopted to designate the men who held this position. A gilt wreath with silver lighting bolts was also prescribed for the 1895-pattern forage cap. *USA*

Opposite page, top:
Another 1899 addition came in the form of a new drab campaign hat, in this case one that had a large screen vent for air circulation on either side of the crown, as worn here by men of Troop E, Seventh U.S. Cavalry. The previous 1889 pattern campaign hat had a perforated vent that had been found wanting. *JMC*

Opposite page, bottom: Although, as of 1899, the official enlisted man's khaki blouse was to have a falling collar, many officers continued to have stand collar jackets, as does the second lieutenant seated in the center of the front row of Troop E, Seventh U.S. Cavalry. *JMC*

Right: These light artillerymen still wear the 1889-pattern campaign hat, although they were photographed after the turn of the century. A lag period between the discontinuation of old patterns and adoption of new ones was very common. Note the roll or 'falling' collar on the khaki enlisted blouse that was called for in 1899, replacing the earlier jackets that had stand collars. *UK*

Left: Towards the end of the nineteenth century, however, some officers did avail themselves of the slightly more comfortable falling collar. Indeed, the young second lieutenant seated in the center of the front row and a few other comrades in this group picture have falling collars, although most wear the stand collar version. The variations in the shades of khaki are likewise evident here. Three of the officers also appear in the 1895-pattern dark blue wool officer's blouse with concealed buttons. *NA*

Opposite page, bottom: By 1899 uniform regulations provided for a range of shirts, including dark-blue flannel ones in light or heavy quality cloth, as worn by the man with the guitar at his lap; and chambray shirts (interwoven blue and white cotton threads), which most of these bandsmen wear except for the one with the striped civilian shirt and the man in the khaki blouse. *FSHM*

Below: Men of Troop E, Seventh U.S. Cavalry, fire a volley over the grave of Private George Reininger, the first man of the unit to die after the unit arrived at their station in 1902 at Pinar, Philippines. The troop commander, Captain E.B. Fuller, tips his non-regulation private purchase straw hat in a final salute. Such headgear was often obtained by officers and men in tropical climates. Fuller also has the white trousers and matching white 1895-pattern officer's jacket.

Above: In 1900, when the international relief expedition was mounted for China, men of the Sixth U.S. Cavalry formed part of the American contingent. They arrived in their dark blue blouse, sky-blue trousers, and drab campaign hats or 1895-pattern forage caps. Some of the officers of Troop L halted at the Avenue of Statues near the Ming tombs, outside Peking, wear the ulster overcoat. Others in the group seem to have 1883-pattern brown canvas, blanket lined overcoats. *NA*

Below: Fourteenth U.S. Infantry foot soldiers typified the two-tone appearance of the late nineteenth century when 1883-pattern blue flannel shirts were combined with khaki trousers, as seen here during the 1900 Boxer Rebellion in China. *USAMHI*

Opposite page, top: On 14 August 1900 men of the Fourteenth U.S. Infantry march along the outer defenses of Peking in the old blue wool uniform. These foot soldiers would scale the Tartar Wall to reach the besieged legations. *USAMHI*

Opposite page, bottom: The blanket roll and campaign hat cord are in evidence as men of the Fourteenth Infantry come to the aid of the besieged legations in Peking in August 1900. *USAMHI*

Above: After defeating the Chinese forces, men of the Fourteenth U.S. Infantry returned to the Philippines where the unit's color guard posed for posterity. By this time the khaki summer uniform had been widely distributed to troops serving outside the United States. Note the special 1884-pattern color belt and sling provided for the color sergeant (left).

Below: On 15 August 1900 Battery F, commanded by Captain Henry Reilly, blasted down the gates of the Forbidden City, in one of the final actions to quell the Boxer Rebellion. A British officer can be seen in the right foreground observing the American gunners in their khaki uniforms manning 3.2-inch 'bag guns.' *NA*

Above: Adna R. Chaffee, Sr., a regular army officer who had been promoted to the rank of major general of volunteers, was given command of the U.S. forces sent to China in 1900. He stands, front and center, with his staff wearing the khaki uniform associated with volunteers, his cuffs, collar, and shoulder loops being covered in dark blue for his position as a staff officer. Most of the other men appear in the typical khaki uniform of regulars with only the shoulder loops being faced in branch colors. On the right a Fourteenth U.S. Infantry officer wears the 1895-pattern officer's jacket. To his right another officer has on the 1898-pattern serge officer's service blouse. Finally, the man in the white 1880-pattern officer's summer helmet wears the complete 1898-pattern summer uniform. *NA*

Right: The block style 'U.S.' insignia and crossed sabers with regimental numbers continued to be positioned on the collar of the 1895-pattern officer's blouse. These could be gilt metal or embroidered in gold. This jacket could be worn with the 1895-pattern officer's forage cap depicted here or the campaign hat. This photo was taken after the establishment of the Fourteenth U.S. Cavalry in 1900, as part of yet another increase in the size of the army following the Spanish-American War. *USCM*

Above: In 1901 loops were added to the 1895-pattern white officer's jacket upon which insignia of rank and a gilt metal Arms of the United States could be placed for all officers below the rank of colonel (except second lieutenants who were to have only the Arms of the U.S.) while the collar was to bear pin-backed crossed cannons and regimental number for artillerymen, following the arrangement that had been adopted for the 1898-pattern khaki officer's blouse. The single bar indicates that this officer is a first lieutenant, while the number 2 designates the Second U.S. Artillery. *UK*

Right: Another 1901 initiative instituted a short-lived new dress uniform for officers in the Corps of Engineers, including collar and cuff ornamentation of bullion lace accented by red and white borders, and shoulder knots with a red center on which appeared the engineer castle insignia. This uniform was the predecessor for the 1902-pattern officer's full dress coat. Note the special engineer buttons and the new model saber that would become the universal edged weapon for U.S. Army officers in 1902. *FAM*

Opposite page:
Another change instituted in 1901 was the replacement of the red cross with a green Maltese cross trimmed in white as the insignia for medical department personnel. Medical officers had been instructed to display the Maltese cross as their insignia half a decade earlier. *USA*

Left: Although the men of Troop E, Seventh U.S. Cavalry, look less formal than the young engineer lieutenant in his dress regalia on the previous page, these horsemen nevertheless appear dapper in their chambray shirts and black neckties, mixing both campaign and garrison elements. *JMC*

Above: The late 1880s' medium brown canvas leggings gradually began to give way to light khaki colored versions, as this Eighth U.S. Cavalry private illustrates. The leggings are worn with mounted reinforced blue kersey trousers and the dark blue wool blouse. The khaki Mills belt has loops for revolver ammunition on the right side, and a double row of loops around the remainder of the belt for .30-40 caliber Krag cartridges. *USCM*

Above: The Krag carbine and .38 caliber Colt double-action revolver had become the basic weapons of the cavalry at the end of the Victorian era. These weapons are secured in a rack at the end of the barracks for Troop A, Fourteenth U.S. Cavalry, where some of the members of that unit posed in 1901. *UK*

Below: Khaki webbed cartridge belts made exclusively for carrying revolver ammunition were also provided, as worn by these men from the Twentieth Battery of Artillery. In 1901 the abolition of regiments and the reorganization of all artillery units into batteries or companies of light and heavy artillery required new insignia for the 1895-pattern cap, as shown by the man standing far right and the one kneeling in the center. *UK*

Above: At the end of 1902 a major uniform change was promulgated that called for numerous new patterns, although a number of previously issued items remained in service, such as the 1895-pattern forage cap and all the other nineteenth century items still in use by men of Company E, Twenty-fifth U.S. Infantry, around 1903. Only the small chevrons worn points up by the sergeant seated in the second row far left are of the new 1902 pattern. *FSM*

Right: Although denied the glory of commanding the U.S. expedition to Cuba, Lieutenant General Nelson Miles served as the commanding general of the United States Army during a time of considerable transition. He designed a special uniform for himself in this role – one that would serve as a model for the new 1902-pattern general officer's dress. Miles is seen here in that uniform, while his standard bearer and the others around him wear the full dress that had been regulation from *circa* 1885 through the early twentieth century. *WCC*

A gray-haired sergeant of engineers wears the new 1902-pattern scarlet piped in white chevrons on his *circa* 1895 blouse and retains the 1895-pattern forage cap with brass castle bearing the designation of Company A. *FAM*